A Boy, a Mouse, and a Spider

The Story of E. B. White

BARBARA HERKERT ✦ illustrated by LAUREN CASTILLO

Christy Ottaviano Books

HENRY HOLT AND COMPANY
NEW YORK

Henry Holt and Company, *Publishers since 1866*
Henry Holt® is a registered trademark of Macmillan Publishing Group, LLC
175 Fifth Avenue, New York, New York 10010 • mackids.com

Image in the author's note: E. B. White, New York, 1948
Photograph by Irving Penn © Condé Nast

Library of Congress Cataloging-in-Publication Data
Names: Herkert, Barbara, author. | Castillo, Lauren, illustrator.
Title: A boy, a mouse, and a spider : the story of E. B. White /
Barbara Herkert ; illustrated by Lauren Castillo.
Other titles: Story of E. B. White
Description: First edition. | New York : Christy Ottaviano Books /
Henry Holt and Company, 2017. | Includes bibliographical references.
Identifiers: LCCN 2016050877 | ISBN 978-1-62779-245-5 (hardcover)
Subjects: LCSH: White, E. B. (Elwyn Brooks), 1899–1985. | Authors,
American—20th century—Biography. | Children's stories—Authorship.
Classification: LCC PS3545.H5187 Z685 2017 | DDC 818/.5209 [B]—dc23
LC record available at https://lccn.loc.gov/2016050877

Our books may be purchased in bulk for promotional, educational, or business use.
Please contact your local bookseller or the Macmillan Corporate and Premium Sales Department
at (800) 221-7945 ext. 5442 or by e-mail at MacmillanSpecialMarkets@macmillan.com.

First edition, 2017 / Designed by Patrick Collins
The artist used brown ink, Adobe Photoshop, watercolor, and foam print textures
on Arches hot pressed paper to create the illustrations for this book.
Printed in China by RR Donnelley Asia Printing Solutions Ltd., Dongguan City, Guangdong Province

1 3 5 7 9 10 8 6 4 2

When young Elwyn White
lay sick in bed,
a bold house mouse
befriended him.
Elwyn made a home
for his companion.
If Mother knew,
she would not approve.

Elwyn tucked
his fearless comrade
in the pocket
of his sailor suit.
The pair conducted
dusty expeditions
to the attic . . .

. . . and musky inspections
of the horse barn.

In the refuge of the stable,
Elwyn's senses sharpened
to the ripe scent of manure,
the creak of harness leather,
the perfect shape of eggs,
the snort of tired horses,
the sweet-dry smell of hay,
and a spider's masterpiece.

When the time came
for kindergarten,
shy Elwyn fought
with all his might.
Noooo! I won't go!
His parents persisted.

Elwyn now sat
in a spotless linen suit,
fretting over his fears.
What if Miss Greene
called on him?
What if he had to use
the dreaded basement bathroom?
Where was his mouse friend?

Every day after school,
Elwyn's collie, Mac,
escorted him home.
Elwyn tossed his books
and bounded for the barn,

where pigeons, snakes, polliwogs,
caterpillars, chameleons, rabbits,
turtles, and canaries he collected
lived in cages, coops, and jars.

As Elwyn grew,
he surveyed the summer stars.
His ears captured
an owl's query,
the breeze's beckoning,
the scuffing of horse hooves.
He jotted his reflections
in a journal.
Writing what he saw, heard, and felt
made him feel free.
I wonder what I might be . . .

Each day,
Elwyn recorded
his praise of the world.
His poem "To a Mouse"
won a prize.

The blank page called to Elwyn.
Writing filled him with joy.
This is where I belong.

In college,
Elwyn wrote clear headlines
and dashing truths
for the *Cornell Daily Sun.*
Friends nicknamed him Andy.
As editor in chief,
he submerged himself
in printer's ink.
Words were Andy's world.

A mouse appeared to Andy
on a train one night in a dream.
The dapper chap
was completely dressed
with a hat and cane.
Another courageous mouse
had entered Andy's life,
a mouse named Stuart Little.

When he came home for the holidays,
eighteen nieces and nephews
begged Andy for a story.
He spun Stuart's tales
for his eager audience.
At every visit back
to Summit Avenue,
Andy added episodes
of the mouse-boy's quest.

After college,
Andy worked for
The New Yorker magazine.
He married Katharine,
an editor he met there.
They soon became a family—
Nancy, Roger, and baby Joel.
Amid the raucousness of the city,
Andy longed for a farm,
a high-lofted barn
filled with animals and hay.

Like a piper,
he led his little family
toward his dream in Maine.

Andy filled his barn
with stoic sheep,
anxious hens,
and gossiping geese.
But he still had a mouse
on his mind.

He followed his instincts
and turned his mouse stories
into a book, *Stuart Little.*

Andy repaired a roof
while another story brewed inside him.
He raised a pig and wondered,
what if the creature was rescued
from a farmer's deadly plan?

In an old boathouse,
with a mouse for company,
Andy tapped out his ideas.
But who would be the story's hero?

One cold October evening,
Andy watched a spider spin.
He climbed a ladder
for a closer look.
He'd found the hero of his story—
Charlotte A. Cavatica.
She rewove destiny with words.
In the gleaming strands of her web,
Charlotte formed the bond
of friendship.

E. B. White
celebrated life through
a mouse's journey,
the pact between a pig and a spider,
and the power of words.
He basked in the seasons,
the peace of the barn,
the beauty of the world.
His stories capture
the glory of nature
and the comfort of hope.

E. B. White, New York, 1948
Photograph by Irving Penn © Condé Nast

AUTHOR'S NOTE

Elwyn Brooks White was born on July 11, 1899 (7/11, a "lucky day"), in Mount Vernon, New York, the youngest of six children. The sprawling gray-and-white house on Summit Avenue was the setting for his early explorations—from the curious collection of birds' eggs in an attic cabinet to the ripe world of the stable behind the house.

As a child, Elwyn was small and sickly. His hay fever was so severe that his father took the family to Maine every August for the fresh coastal air. There, Elwyn explored the shores of Great Pond in an Old Town canoe. Boats would forever fascinate him as a symbol of freedom.

School was not for Elwyn, as he suffered from a myriad of fears—fear of the dark, fear of the future, fear of public speaking, fear of failure. He found solace in the many animals he kept as pets. Elwyn started writing at a very early age. Expressing what he saw, heard, and felt gave him a sense of achievement in his boisterous household. He kept a journal and wrote in it every day.

At Cornell University, he acquired the name "Andy" and wrote news stories and headlines for the college newspaper. There, he met Professor William Strunk Jr., author of the self-published pamphlet on the basics of writing well, *The Elements of Style*. Andy would revise his late professor's book in 1957 under his pen name, E. B. White. The book is still widely used by students and professional writers.

Following college, Andy took a trip west in a Model T Ford with his friend Howard "Cush" Cushman. Like his favorite author, Henry David Thoreau,

Andy desired freedom, "to hear what was in the wind." Years later, his fictional hero, Stuart Little, would take a similar journey.

After stints at United Press, the American Legion News Service, and *The Seattle Times*, Andy settled into a job at *The New Yorker* magazine. There he met his future wife, Katharine, an editor at the magazine. Although he enjoyed writing "Notes and Comment" for *The New Yorker*, Andy felt that he hadn't produced anything of real importance yet.

He first saw the farm in Maine that would become their home in 1933. There was the barn that *Charlotte's Web* would make famous. From Maine, he wrote a series of essays for *Harper's Magazine* that would be published later as the book *One Man's Meat*.

Stuart Little, E. B. White's first children's book, was published in 1945. Stuart, the mouse who had appeared in a dream, had many of the author's attributes—his love of boats, cars, skating, and travel; his love of morning and summertime.

E. B. wrote much of *Charlotte's Web* in the boathouse of his farm in Maine. He had made up his mind to write a children's book about animals and he felt he needed a way to save a pig's life. He found his spider hero, Charlotte, spinning an egg sac in an outbuilding. In the character of Fern, E. B. imbued characteristics he'd had as a boy: Fern loved early morning, and she loved animals, like he did. The book was an instant sensation when it was published in 1952 and remains widely popular to this day.

E. B. wrote his third and final children's book in 1968, *The Trumpet of the*

Swan. Again, the author revealed glimpses of himself. Again, he shared his wonder of the world.

E. B. White received many awards during his lifetime, including a Newbery Honor for *Charlotte's Web* in 1953, the Presidential Medal of Freedom in 1963, the Laura Ingalls Wilder Medal in 1970, the National Medal for Literature in 1971, and a special citation from the Pulitzer Prize jury in 1978. His beloved classics are forever reaching new generations of readers.

BIBLIOGRAPHY

Elledge, Scott. *E. B. White: A Biography*. New York: W. W. Norton & Company, 1985.

Sims, Michael. *The Story of Charlotte's Web: E. B. White's Eccentric Life in Nature and the Birth of an American Classic*. New York: Walker & Company, 2011.

White, E. B. *Essays of E. B. White*. New York: Harper Perennial, 1977.

White, E. B., edited by Dorothy Lobrano Guth and Martha White. *Letters of E. B. White*. New York: Harper Perennial, 2007.

White, Martha, ed. *E. B. White on Dogs*. Gardiner, Maine: Tilbury House Publishers, 2013.

White, Martha, ed. *In the Words of E. B. White*. Ithaca, New York: Cornell University Press, 2011.